POETRY:
TO YOUR HEART
FROM MINE

POETRY:
TO YOUR HEART
FROM MINE

John Warren Owen

To order additional copies of this book, contact:
Xlibris Corporation
1-888-795-4274
www.Xlibris.com
Orders@Xlibris.com
26213

CONTENTS

FEELINGS

PAST, PRESENT, AND FUTURE

HUMOR AND WHIMSY

ROMANCE AND PASSION

PHILOSOPHY AND BEAUTY

ACKNOWLEDGEMENTS

I, John Warren Owen, wish to herewith especially thank the following persons for their assistance, advice and encouragement in my poetic efforts:

Mary Billie Crano-Crosley, whose own poetic artistry made her contributions, critiques and assistance all the more worthwhile;

Mary Norma Goodwin Owen and Pamela Anne Owen Silverio for their assistance and encouragement;

My many online fellow poet friends for their individual poems and ideas for poetry subjects;

And, most of all, my dear parents, Charles William and Lena Clara Koehler Owen, for providing the genes that have allowed me my poetic expression.

FEELINGS

LIFE IS PRECIOUS

Life is precious when in love,
and time is precious from above;
to pass through life without a pause
and give us cause to treasure, savor,
grasp it close—the time and so the love.
Hold them here,
hold them dear,
lest the life, the love,
both disappear.

MY FAVORITE EMOTION

Greed, hate, pity,
sympathy, empathy, care,
who's to choose amongst them,
choose with soul laid bare?

Is your "favorite" one
who does you favors?
I think rather it's the one
you look upon with favor—
even savor—as in *love*.

Love sits above them all;
the emotion in whose devotion
we frequently are basking
without asking for the greatest
shining from above—love.

Draw it onto you and cling
to everything it offers
from out its coffers,
lest it feel neglect,
and when you least expect,
like a dove take its love
and fly away.

MY UNEARTHLY FRIENDS

They are the someones who watch over me.
They save me from catastrophe.
They soothe my soul.
They seem forever at my beck and call,
   and give their all to protect, defend me,
   keep me safe when danger's imminent,
   and night and day they're at my right hand.
What grand plan represents they
   in their day-by-day availability?
Tranquility covers me when I think on their presence.
Their essence is love—to me.

O my dear ones,
   you, who far from space
   take your places in my heart,
   always part of my coming,
   of my going,
   of my misgivings, my mistakes,
   and all the mysteries of my existence
   looked upon with your insistence
   that my being's being well.

No hell have they.
I only pray with body bent
   that they may all be heaven-sent.
I thank whatever God and gods abide
   that they be ever at my side.

My guardian angels that you are,
   come down to me from God's bright star
   to let me know how dear you are to me
   on this, my terminating sea.

DESIRE

I want to get in touch with life,
I want to tread its ways;
I want to feel its storm and strife,
and hold its nights and days.

I want its waves to wash o'er me,
and bathe my body clean;
and help me meet the heav'nly hills
and depths I've never seen.

Life's music haunts my heart and soul,
and makes my spirits rise;
its beauty lifts me toward my goal
wherein my future lies.

If I should reach that holy grail,
that grail that all men seek;
I hope to live to tell the tale,
of which my spirits speak.

HEARD AT CONCERT

As I hear the voices,
I think not of the Christ child,
but of the voices
of my dear departed sons,
singing with me,
singing of the Christ,
the Santa, the winter,
the joy, jubilance,
the days, the years long gone,
and I start a tear or two
in fond thought,
fond happening,
fond memory—
overwhelming fondness
cov'ring me
like the winter snow to come.

A WALK THRU THE WOODS

The woods are especially
beautifully satisfying
on a rainy autumn day.
Their leaves turning in color,
smiling at you thru their drip,
catching your eye, body,
even lip, tongue
as you sip.

The woods demand you walk slowly
thru their splendor.

Splendor,
that's it!

No wonder poets wrote
of stopping in the woods
to catch their magic.

They knew,
too.

DANCING FLAMES

They dance, they entice,
they excite,
they entreat me
to feel their warmth
even to burning!

Thoughts a'churning,
wond'ring, conjecturing,
the thrill of the dance,
shadows jumping,
flick'ring across the bowers
of my conscience,
arousing my stifled embers,
threat'ning my semi-complacency,
painting my pallid countenance
with dancing imag'ry.

SUMMER RAIN

Summer rain can be a blessing
or a bane.
The pool is closed
with lightning flashing,
thunder crashing,
guards are closing gates
while teeth are gnashing
at the kill-joy climate.

But then the scene is changed
when good old Sol comes forth amain,
and swimmers dive the pool again,
and grateful grasses lick their lips,
and bless the blessed rain.

TENDERNESS AND FIRE

Tenderness and fire, together?
Yes—within DESIRE.
When the will and want are quickened,
heart's AFIRE!
There's a tenderness that enters in
that want and will require,
and requiring, set in motion
thoughts and feelings
and desire that's interposed,
interposed into a notion that
has not yet been disclosed,
but that will be soon in future,
when the flame and touch are one,
and the reticence that once was
has receded, ebbed, and gone.

UP FROM DOWN

Everything's on hold.
What better than
to be held,
be comforted,
be caressed
when "down"?

We should be so lucky.

Down in the dumps we take our lumps
and always come back for more.
But how good it is,
that "hold,"
that man would trade his gold
for the touch, the care,
that's known
when "down"?
We revel in it,
wallow in it,
and we give thanks
for that caress
that soothes stress,
that clears the frown
when "down."

MY FAVORITE TOY

My favorite toy is my little boy imagination
and I savor it.
Play with it as I will, it never shows signs of wear,
and remains in its little niche until I literally itch
to call upon it,
whereupon it promptly and dutifully answers
"I am here!"

I sometimes toy with ideas that many would eschew
because they might be new to those whose imaginations
lie close to stagnation; but never the mind,
since finally we all wind up at the same destination.

I love to travel,
and, boy! my little toy takes me on trips
I could never pay for
without my tiny toy
to let me have my joy with him,
and let my longings unravel.

Okay, my little boy toy,
come now into my reckoning,
and take my hand and lead me
to far-off lands a'beckoning.

SPICE

Add a little spice to your life!
Pepper or romance, chance it.
It will make all the difference,
and what differs and interests, enhances,
makes the chances worthwhile,
brings a smile from glumness.

Spice gives rise to zest,
and zest rewards the quest
for the out-of-the-ordinary,
the exciting, the inviting,
the deliciousness of diversion.

So taste and see how nice it is
to use a little pinch of spice
to lift you up from stress and strife
to zestful life!

SAVOR THE MOMENT

We'll savor the love that was given us,
and be thankful for all that has driven us
to knowing this stage
of a lover's next page
that keeps growing
and never stops flowing between us;
reminding us never
to sever the bond
that these moments will last
for the now,
and beyond.

REVERIE

Silky, filmy, lovely thoughts
filled my brain.
Warmness within.
Wishing, wanting those
wispy love whispers
I'd dreamed about,
schemed about
in my midnight reverie.

So up I got,
and down I went
to the TV
still flick'ring from
the night before's mysteries.
Now I'd get some *real* pictures,
in place of my gauzy,
nocturnal bed imagines.

What?
No hints at even romance,
even suggestiveness?
Click by click channels flashed by.
Comedy, history, biography, science,
all I didn't want.
So back up I go.

Pillow-hugging will have to do
for this night's escapade.

ALL JAZZED UP

When you're "all jazzed up,"
you've been improvised,
taken liberties with
that can be good
and that can be bizarre,
dependent upon
how "wised up" you are.

If you're wise, you'll improvise,
so that your version
is better than the original.
You'll forget the formal
and create something new
to view or to listen to.

But be careful.
Too much "jazzing up"
will be like drinking too many cups of wine
and may end you up a little out of line
with all that jazz.

IN THE KEY OF BLUE

Some songs are sung blue.
So who's singin' the blues?
Such a pretty hue
to be connected to
"feelin' blue."

Blues songs arise out of sadness,
nostalgia, loss of something or someone,
depression of mind, body, or wealth,
poor health, lost love.

A simple song, simply sung, deeply felt,
venting the singer's whole,
brought from heart and soul,
bemoaning loneliness,
a soulful song of longing.

And all the while,
behind the song
wails a horn,
playing along
in the key of blue.

UP ABOVE

Fleecy, billowy,
wispy, willowy
clumps of cumulus
clouds.
Snowy white
against a pure-blue
sky.

Thankfully I see them again,
drench myself in the cooling water,
back to bottom,
drinking in the wondrous
scene.

How many millions toil
beneath it all,
without an eye turned upward,
to saturate themselves
with the beauty o'er them?

I did through years,
horizontally oriented,
waging war against want
and seeming deprivation.

O! That someone, something
had given me a demonstration,
an earlier inoculation
with the love
of the omnipresent
"up above."

UNEARTHED REGRET

I said that I had no regrets—
I lied.
There's one regret I surely have
that cannot be denied.
I left my mother in her age alone,
and that's a sin for which I can't atone.

She suckled me, then nursed me,
loved me through my life,
so here, regret, raise up your ugly head
and let me love my mother
'though she's dead.

BENEATH

It's seldom that I feel this way—
down.
My spirits seldom go this way—
down.
I must have something in my craw,
or deep down in my mind,
that causes consternation 'bout
a thing that I can't find,
way
deep
down.
Won't someone, something, come along
and raise my spirits up?
I'd pay a pretty penny, maybe,
out of beggars' cup
for someone, something, who could hear
my helpless moans and cries
and come and rescue me
from memory
that tears
and blurs
my eyes.

IN THE RAIN

I love it in the rain.
Summer, winter, fall, or spring,
I love the feel of it, the sound of it,
the smell of it, the spell of it.

A tingling of the blood occurs
when out in it
especially when drops strike the hair,
dripping down over the eyelids,
moistening the mouth,
on their watery way
to saturation satisfaction.

O when will it rain,
and let me savor it all again?

FROM FEAR TO HOPE TO STRENGTH TO RESOLVE

There was no warning.
There was no escaping,
no avoiding, thwarting;
hearts leapt, both inside
and outside the planes.

And then, after a time,
fear set in.
What next? What pretext
would set terror back into action?
What error of judgment,

what diabolical, maniacal
trick of circumstance
would spoil someone's chance
for survival in an upset world?

So now entereth hope,
now entereth resignation,
now entereth strength of will
to endure the scourge
of the urge to evil.

Time, both friend and foe,
passes by,
as a world
evolving,
steels itself in readiness,
resolving.

'NEATH IT ALL

When many serpents rear their heads
they can be so demanding
that drastic measures thwart a few
and leave the others standing.

A reptile isn't slimy,
although it might be cold,
but underneath that sleekened skin
may lie a heart of gold.

So tend the heart and feel the skin
and let the serpent know
that underneath it all there lies
a love that will not go.

LITTLE GIRL

I will write a poem about a child.

Baby Jesus, meek and mild,
is not of ilk so sweet and saucy,
even naughty, apt to bilk you
out of anything you have within,
so better keep it, goodness, sin,
hidden where this little snout won't
sneak right in, and find you out!

And there she was,
this little imp,
simply acting as she was,
while age looked on
her rosy little cheeks,
little cheeks with
sometimes dimply smile,
and then that look beguiling
all who sat before her,
wond'ring what is next to flip
from pretty, pursed, but ready lip.
Surely she will give us all the slip
and vanish from her sometimes naughty,
sometimes haughty childhood
into wiser womanhood,
with dimples, lips,
so late, so soon,
a'crooning other, tempting tune.

LEST YOU FORGET ME

Lest you forget me,
just remember this:
when I look into your eyes
I'm filled with the brightness of you,
sliding down your beam
into the depths of you,
into your very being,
seeing through your eyes
all that is worth seeing,
hoping beyond all hope
that you see back into mine.

I'm basking in your rays above,
letting your love warm me inside,
while riding a beam down
through your eyes into your heart,
where I remain a part of you,
and you of me,
all leaving my sign
imprinted within you,
lest you forget me,
and that you're mine.

A PLETHORA OF PULCHRITUDE

A plethora of pulchritude is what I saw today.
A plethora is quite a lot,
and pulchritude is what she's got
a'walking up my way.

The world's so full of pulchritude,
no matter clothed or figure nude,
it's all the same when eye's aflame
when beauteousness is nigh,
and cute-eousness whenever all that
pulchritude's apparent to the eye.

Beauty here, beauty there,
beauty, beauty ev'rywhere
drink it in, short of sin,
let your eye explore the skin.

I'll take my chances,
whether on the beach
or at the show,
and sit and watch and wonder
where that beauty has to go
to have the recognition
it so def'nitely deserves,
while we all sit in awe of it,
and treasure ev'ry little bit,
and all consume the beauty food
that we call lovely pulchritude.

FATE

Fate awaits with outstretched arm,
no alarm to sound,
while 'round and 'round the senses go,
rising, falling, searching to and fro
for what the fateful future waits
to fall upon us.

Reach the arms and hands far out,
seek to grasp what lies about our reach;
then sooner fate's strong arm and hand
will draw us out to see
our destiny.

WINTER'S CHILL

I've had my fill of winter's chill.
I think I'll move far south,
to maybe Mexico, and let
those tasty tacos fill my mouth,
and margaritas too, I say,
in very copious measure,
I'll welcome ev'ry sunny day,
and bask in warmth and pleasure.

And when the summer comes around,
I'll travel North, and then,
when winter winds begin to blow,
I'll head back South again.

Old winter's chill's behind me now,
my bones will flex and bend,
so I can take a humble bow
to welcome winter's end.

PAST, PRESENT,
AND
FUTURE

DEAR, DEAR WOMAN

While here, she was not perfect,
but now that she's gone, she is.

She cared for me, both ways.
She cared *about* me
and nursed me through my days.
Through adversity,
through the throes of depression,
through her life, if not through mine.

My dear, dear woman,
would that our paths
would cross again, so fond,
in future, far-off, great beyond.

I'LL SAY GOODBYE TO YESTERDAY

I'll say goodbye to yesterday,
as good as it has been,
and if I live another day,
will never let my sin
prevent me from the beauty of
the life that lies before me,
and the loves and mysteries
that passed my days of yore.

Come to me, day,
and let me lay
my arms about your time,
and grant to me more mystery,
experience sublime.

AT THE MOVIES

I have sat at movies
next to one I loved,
or thought I did,
when just a kid.

I have felt the burning
of the yearning
just to touch her hand,
thereby her heart,
bringing hers to mine.

O to capture back
those days of rapture!

AN AWAKENING

And all of a sudden in life it begins,
you forget all your sorrows,
forget all your sins,
and bask in the glories that once passed you by,
the moon and the earth, the stars and the sky,
the lovers you've loved, the friends here and gone,
the daffodils, daisies, the good times passed on,
and on the horizon, so wond'rously clear,
the feeling of fateness,
your future is here!

BOYHOOD MEMORY

Oh!
How I remember September, December,
the color-soaked trees of the fall in their splendor,
the BRRRRR! of the trudge through the snow,
with hand and toe tender.

Dear Mama saved dinner and served
instead of the butt-beat her darling deserved.

Oh nature, continue revealing your light,
as dreams of my childhood
slip by through the night.

MY OTHER MOTHER

She's the one who spanked me.
She's the one who yanked me by the ear.
She's the one who taught me
how to fear a mother's hand,
taught me how to stand at attention,
how to listen, and then to understand
that my frolic and my colic
were *her* responsibilities, not mine,
and if I was possessed of any spine,
I would do as mother told me,
and then everything would
be
just
fine!

A WALK BACK TO YESTERDAYS

I want to walk.
No hurry.
Walk and watch.
Try to watch the days go by,
or the weeks, months,
more likely the years,
but take in as much yesterday as I can,
savoring, sampling, trying to relive
the joys, accomplishments, even the tears,
forgetting the disappointments, trials
and tragedies that mar my journey
back through manhood
into an idyllic childhood,
loved, loving, and beloved, and
now thankful for the opportunity
to walk back through my yesterdays.

MOMENTS OF MEM'RY

I still remember you.

Your smell,
as I fell for you,
with you,
to you.

Your feel,
as I knelt to you,
begged of you
your love.

Your grasp,
as I clasped
my arms about you,
pulling you
and your lovely wholeness
unto me.

and then,

Your kiss,
melding all of this
into one,
sweet,
sensuous,
wondrous,
willing moment
of remembrance.

STARS

Stars speak remoteness,
stars speak of love,
stars mark the glories
that live up above.
Welcome their beauty,
savor their shine,
call to them softly,
tell them
"be mine."

THE COLORS OF AUTUMN

Some are dull, some are brilliant.
What makes the difference?
Certainly the weather,
the amount of rainfall,
the genus of tree,
but perhaps most importantly,
the eye of the beholder.

The familiar saw, adage, saying is
"beauty is in the eyes of the beholder."
Surely, one who has never experienced
the splendor of autumn color
might well be as impressed with the less brilliant
as is the seasoned savorer of the more brilliant.
Maverick observer or veteran viewer,
there is always striking beauty
in the colors of autumn.

EERIE NIGHT

That night called HALLOWEEN,
it's seen but once a year—officially,
but let me make it clear that
it could come when least supposed,
and tweak both nose and toes opposed,
as well as let you taste of specter's nectar,
summ'ning you to ghostly goblin's table,
set of ghouly gastronomic goulash,
where you can hash
and rehash all you're fed
of eerie, slightly queery,
mostly ghostly happenings abed
throughout the night,

in dreaming fright,
until the light of dawn,
when, grimly, all those
ghastly,
ghouly
ghosts
are gone.

KEEPING IN TOUCH

In touch with reality
more and more,
is enough to make the spirits soar.
I've learned to touch the flowers,
to test their filmy, flimsy texture,
allowing their feel to permeate me
tactilely, olfactorily;
is taste next?

O to awaken to once-forsaken senses,
finding the sight, the sound, the smell,
sensitivities lain dormant, but ever accessible
in the flower of creation.
O taste,
and see.

MEMORIES OF 2001

As time slips by, memories accumulate.

When considering the accumulation
of the year AD 2001, what's done is done,
and lives for borrowed time in memory.

As with all years,
life, love, languish, laughter,
all have their scene,
and what is seen as futile now
may well end up as question, "How?"
and soon be done.

Perpetrated perfidy, treachery,
calamity of nine eleven
stands out, amidst our wince,
above all else as martyred memory,
eclipsing those before or since.

So now an endless task is taken on,
and searching bomb and gun
may be the muddled memories
of AD 2001.

THE GATE

Sometimes it's locked,
sometimes ajar,
ofttimes flung far open,
invitingly.

But who dares enter?
Who to break the lock;
who to even force it open from ajar;
and who the foolhardy, the gutful,
the devil-may-care, to stride straight in
to sanctimony or to sin?

No soul knows until that moment of truth, when,
standing set just outside its confines,
the mind races to meet decision,
and perhaps, just perhaps,
wheels around
and walks away.

FUTILITY

All is futile.
Or so it sometimes seems.

What *is* futile?
Hopeless?
Beyond all help?
Beyond all comprehension?
Beyond *all*?

We must consult the sages of old
and see what they had to say of it.
They well might say that unproductive, fruitless,
fit the mold.

Ah yes, O wise ones, let us have
at least a glimpse of your ability
to tell us what describes futility.

And they might answer, "*Life!*"

Life's never-ending strife's a futile task,
those bygone seers might say,
so save your ask, and take to task
those who would spoil your day.
The clock's all set, and you will get
your time, no matter it's how brutal,
and after all have answered call,
you'll find again,
it's futile.

Study it, plumb it, wish on it,
break your ev'ry bone on it,
and then lie back,
and summ'ning all ability,

give up,

in favor of

futility.

HUMOR
AND
WHIMSY

OUTSIDE MY WINDOW

What is that outside my window?
It appears to be a bird,
but how absurd,
since it well could be a longing.

On second chance perchance
I'm thinking it might be a rabbit.
But could instead it really be a habit
to which I've now become addicted,
fixing everything before me like I want it?

So, dagnabit, someone tell me
what I'm looking at outside,
so that I'm no longer hiding
with my wary wits akimbo,
all the while while I'm a'trying
to look out my wishful window.

AN UNCOMFORTABLE SILENCE

Shhhh!
Someone hears!

Hush!
Someone nears.

I'm uncomfortable
without sound.
Cricket, hound,
rattle of railroad,
her approaching,

space encroaching,
anything to make me well,
anything to break the spell
of this uncomfortable silence.

Hear it?

Shhh!

DON'T BE COY

Don't be coy, you little boy,
let it out, whisper, shout,
just tell it like it is,
then Mama will be proud
her little boy has told it all
out loud.

If you've got a hankering,
tell your Mama,
but you gotta be prepared
for spankering!

I FELL IN LOVE WITH
TEDDY TODAY

I fell in love with Teddy today,
she's only eleven, you know,
but when not in school,
but with me in the pool,
she makes my strong swim strokes seem slow.

I swam the full length underwater,
she watched me, 'midst her dimpled grin,
and then she dove into the shallow,
and swam to the deep, sans breathe in!

I challenged her as I swam farther,
and that's when my love had its start,
for with dimpled laugh trailing,
she dove off the railing,
and swam her way into my heart.

DADDY DOES IT AGAIN

Mama! Mama!
Daddy's done it again!

He spilled the beans,
he ripped his jeans,
he messed the floor,
he slammed the door!

Poor Daddy does the little things
that make the kiddies crow,
whilst sowing seed
to bring another up to grow,
while fam'ly life goes on and up,
with splintered sash and old chipped cup,
and mama always keeping watch
for kiddies comfort, Daddy's blotch!

Daddy! Daddy!
Do it again,
so we can laugh,
and watch the life you live,
with all of us forgiving you
for all the dear things
daddies do!

TWO FROGS

There were two frogs,
not dogs but frogs,
who made their homes in various logs,
and always in those logs was found
a nasty kind of moss
that brought sure death to all who'd toss
the slightest bit deep down their throats,
as if were eating cans, like goats,
but giving up the mastication
for a form of gulp-ulation frogs are prone to do
to anything that strikes their view and fancy.

So these aforesaid frogs were tantalized
by soggy froggy moss,
and tossed some down,
which thereupon caused such a frown
to pass across their jowls,
that there were immediately howls
escaping from their throats.

You say you think they joked?

Think hard!

You know.

They CROAKED!

A DAY IN THE LIFE OF A BUM

Ho hum.
What am I, the bum, to do today?
Ride the rails like yesterday?
Naw, that gets old, and anyway,
ain't no gold in empty boxcars
'long the way,
with other hoboes and their snores
to take up half their hours
to nowhere.

Maybe I can get some stew or somethin' more
if I go knock on lady's door
who'll see the sorrow in my eye
and hand me piece o' punkin' pie, and say
"Now, bum, you have a happy day!"

The woods will always offer
day's or nighttime's peace and grub,
and place for itchy back's fine rub against a tree,
and so I watch from train for likely lane
to take to dark seclusion, just for me.

My matches light an evening fire
from twigs and logs always nearby,
and boughs can make a nice soft lie
when sun and passing thoughts are done.

Ho hum,
so ends this day for bum.

A PENNY'S WORTH OF THOUGHT

I saw a penny on the floor,
'twas just inside the open door;
it lay there without care,
without a why or where or want.

It didn't want for any pocket,
it didn't care to be in safe;
the one who picked it up
would never know
how far that penny had to go
to reach its final destination;
and neither would the penny
have any inclination
toward its end-up-ness,
whether in the plate
by church's child,
or by the drunken sot
in night so wild;

and neither ever given thought
to what that mindless
penny bought.

LOST

Lost?
Lost in what?
Lost in thought?
Lost in the woods?
Lost love?

Let's be specific here.
No, on further thought,
let's be general.

When lost, we can't find our way.
Well, what does that say?
To go whichever way the road leads.
If it leads us to "Ys,"
we'll take the road seems
wisest ambulation.
After all, the all is speculation,
so road,
lead on,
and damn the destination!

HALLOWEEN

Halloween, that hallowed night,
when children hold themselves a'fright,
and ghosts and goblins stir about
the neighborhood, inside and out,
and mommies tuck their littles in,
after their daddies bring them in
with bags a'full, and tricks all done,
to then await next morning's sun
arising on another day
to eagerly awake and say
"I'm gonna count my treats and gum,
and wait another hallowed day to come!"

FLIES

Flies are fast!
In the twinkling of your eye
one has flown and said, "Bye-bye,"
flying toward the sky or ceiling,
or toward the pie upon the table,

free of fly contamination,
until it's made his destination
and his hatchery;
what abomination!

Folded newsprints finally exceed fly speed,
ending all the consternation,
and regeneration with it.

Have you ever sat in wait
for a fly to come and sit,
and swat and swat and swat and swat
until he sits and seems to smile and say,
"Have done with it!"

WHEN I FINISH GROWING UP

When I finish growing up,
I'll probably grow down,
and all my friends and family
will look at me and frown,
and say, "Poor man, please tell us what
has caused your new compression,"
and I will answer, sighing,
"I suffer from depression!"

THOU SHALT NOT WHINE

"Thou shalt not whine" is a line
to say to guests at repasts
while wining and dining,
all finally falling on drunken ears,
on sunken floors.

Then more's the need for
more wining and dining,
and less whining,
while minding one's
manners at meals,

even when one feels
like whining
while dining.

LIKE A BIRD

Let me fly away,
like a bird.

Let me chirp my say,
like a bird.

Cup me in your hands,
like a bird,

visit far-off lands,
like a bird.

And when I have flown my last wing,
let me sing the most beautiful song
a bird has ever heard.

DAILY INFANTORY

There was an old woman
who lived in a shoe,
she had so many children,
she knew not what to do.

She put them in their places
when they all had their way,
and counted heads
when in their beds,
and where each moppet lay.

In concluding this story,
it begs me to say,
she had to take "infantory"
at the end of each day!

ROMANCE
AND
PASSION

A LOSS

If I should leave
I'd surely grieve
for one who cared for me;
for one who cared,
with whom I shared
a tender love that we
had let grow strong
so that no wrong
could never, ever be.

But days and years
add up to tears,
may sweep
our love to sea,
and render dumb
a love that some
would live a life to see.

ABOUT LOVE

Love is many splendored,
I love to say.
Why?
Because it's true!

When you love,
you love in a variety of ways,
all caring, providing,
protecting, consoling—
loving!

But there's one love
amongst the many
that involves an intensity
called desire—
passion!
This one love is the sensual,
sexually-oriented love.
A love involving the mind,
the heart, the viscera,
even the soul,
but primarily the body.
A sensuosity desiring,
nay, demanding
release, satisfaction.
And when this desire exists mutually
between two love-partners,
a union is conceived,
the likes of which
is not to be found
elsewhere.

WHISPERS CAUGHT IN THE WIND

A whisper goes a long way
when wafted windward.
And despite its flimsy, filmy faintness,
can do much good, or considerable harm,
based upon the degree of love or venom
spewed at its outset.

Rumors are whispered conjectures
of whatever true or false origin,
and are capable of
spreading harm afar.

Conversely, whispers of love
can carry ardor, warmth, romance,
as they flit themselves tenderly
through their fanciful flight
from heart to waiting heart.

ALLURE

Allure is a sure pathway to pleasure,
and allure is a sure road to trouble.
But there is good trouble and bad trouble.
Just avoid the bad and double the good!

We should all secure
as many paths to allure
the law and all else allows.

Look beyond the allure,
and see the latch it opens
into a waiting expanse
in which to play and dance
with all the chances taken
with the call of
allure.

DON'T GO

Whenever you leave me
I never want to see you go.
It's then you never fail to grieve me,
I guess it's 'cause I love you so.

Your presence
is like a sweet perfume to me,
your essence
is all I've ever hoped you'd be.

So stay when I cry,
and let us abide
our love shared in two,
invented for you,
to be at my side.

I'D RATHER

I'd rather be monkey who lives in a zoo?
No, for imprisoned by steel bars,
I couldn't find you.
No, rather your loveliness,
rather your grace,
and rather your time-worn
but beautiful face,
and rather those dear things
that dwell in your heart,
the things in your mind
of which I am a part,
and hopefully too,
as I glance at my goal,
a love for me
hidden down deep
in your soul.

SING TO ME

Sing to me a song of love,
    as angels sing from up above,
    and fill my heart with ecstasies
    that live and die with memories,
so I can savor on the 'morrow
    song of yours to ease my sorrow,
    all the hurt that's hurting me,
    leaving all at thy sweet call,
while I listen in elation,
    ridding me of consternation,
setting soul and mind and heart at ease,
    freeing me from savage beast
    with thy sweet voice,
    the least of which
    will let my spirits soar,
    and bring me joy
    forevermore.

FOOLS TOGETHER

Fools together, you and I,
reaching for the heavens,
settling for the sky,
grasping for forever
what only tomorrow will bring,
living for the moment,
making our hearts sing.

What if on the morrow,
song begins to fade,
bringing on a sorrow
man or God has made?

Live it then, the moment,
clasp it to your breast,
let the fading music
satisfy the rest.

A SPECIAL HUNGER

Hunger sets in
when something's missing,
like hugging and kissing,
and other little things
affection brings.

It's hard to satiate
with opiate-like affection,
no matter in which direction
it flows.

So here it goes,
back and forth,
up and down,
inside and outside,
'round and 'round,
never spent
'til two have lent it all,
and wait for call
to renewal.

COME INTO MY HEART

Come into my heart,
there is room for you there;
rid yourself of all sorrow,
dispense with all care;
rest you certain and peaceful,
let a quietude reign, so
that on the morrow
you'll rise up again
with the vigor and spirit
you've had from the start,
when you yielded, surrendered,
and entered my heart.

KISSES NEVER TAKEN BACK

When the mind's alive, aglow,
thoughts a'scatt'ring to and fro,
there's a moment shutting down
all that's happ'ning, smile or frown;

captured moment resting there,
time awaiting action, where,
suddenly, without intent,
hand and head are quickly bent
to the lips of one fair Miss
who desires the fevered kiss
of one who offers, through his lack,
kisses never taken back.

WE

She sat there, and I sat here.
And yet she kept moving toward me,
not physically in motion, but psychically,
spiritually, condescendingly.

What was it I felt?
What movement sensed I?

Our eyes fixed together,
periodically, regularly.
Admiringly?
Certainly on my part.
But where her heart lay
I knew not surely,
but intuitively, even hopefully.

We parted,
something started,
never finished.

THE THINGS OF LOVE

Spit them out, one by one,
   the things of love.
Extricate them from your heart,
   the things of love.
It could be
   that with this above ability
   to count them out,
   the things of love will bare themselves

when given time and inclination,
destination from within, without,
the feeling, caring, touching,
baring all that's lying deep within,
the heart, the mind, the soul,
touching deep, so as to keep
the things of love—.

NATURE'S PALETTE

God's beauty surrounds me,
it glows in the day,
it drives all my cares
and my sorrows away;
it infuses my being,
appeals to my fire,
and plumbs up the depths
of my hidden desire.

Clustered clumps of autumnal color,
painted shades in varied hue,
nature's gift to me and you.

At evening the hues
are as rich as before.
The trees former fire
has recessed into more
of subdued forms of richness
pervading the scene:
you and I and the wonder
of all we have seen.

LIFE LINK

She was a life link to my heart.
We sat alone at night and
counted stars amidst our eyes,
not thinking of goodbyes.

The next day all was still
amid the chill
of unrequited love.
What from above,
or for that matter from below,
could slow departure?

So then I went,
and I was sent a'flying
back to my reality,
but still rememb'ring
all that beauty that was ours
among the stars,
and e'en with parting,
rememb'ring life link
to my heart.

WHEN YOUR LOVER HAS GONE

When you wake with the dawn,
and your lover has gone,
and you lie there forlorn as can be,
a remembrance still clings
to your heart, and it sings a sad song
that you'd just as soon be
caught in some other throe
so your lover won't know
how it hurts with its intensity.

As the days pass you by
you are wondering why
this calamity happened to you;
so you rise up and shine
and reach out for divine
or at least for a self you have lent
to brighten your dawn,
though your lover has gone,
gone with all of the love you have spent.

As the days start to dwindle
you seek to rekindle a spark
that your heart shouldn't spurn,
but the coals just won't glow,
and you finally know
that what once was
will never return.

PHILOSOPHY
AND
BEAUTY

RELIGION?

Religion?
The "opiate of the masses"?
How many classes
do we have to attend
to learn about God?
Is it the Bible today,
the Koran tomorrow,
burning the midnight oil
to find in what soil
the ark lies buried?

Would that God himself
would come down from above
and help us solve his mysteries.
Instead, we look
in ev'ry book and cranny
of the library, to see
if he is hidden there.

What knave like I, Kant
would rant and rave
at midnight hour
along with Schopenhauer?
They knew some answers,
but it would take a month
of Sundays to grind the grist
to just make up the pages missed
while praying on the Sabbath.

Why is it, after spending all our days
absorbing page on page,
we still go on our sinful ways,
religion in our hearts and minds
for which we never pay the wage?
Somewhere it says,

"The wages of sin is death,"
and you can bet we'll get there
sooner or later, Bible and Koran set aside
by those of us who loved and died,
and we seldom the wiser for it.

Religion upon religion,
sung by legions of men,
pursuing and eschewing,
then caught in their foibles
as poor begging mortals,
forgetting the multinumbered things
religion brings.
And so the question remains:
religion?

MY DEDICATION

I am dedicated to music.
I am illuminated by it.

No preoccupation with the mundane,
the ordinary, the vicissitudes of life;
no trials and tribulations,
nor calculations of assets versus liabilities.

Pushing away the daily cares
of everyday existence,
my insistence is upon spending
as much time as is possible
with my unending love—
music!

Unlike many other aspects of living,
music never fails to send back
more in its giving.

Lift your voice in song!
Strike a harmonic chord!
Sing, play your heart away!
And when you feel
there's somethin' real
you're missin'—
LISTEN!

SANCTUARY

I have a sanctuary deep within
where all my thoughts are contained;
it matters not awake, asleep,
nor if let out, restrained.
It lies in satisfaction,
beck'ning me
to let it tell its care,
and other times
lets me decide
who lived,
and put it there.

HER BARENESS

I saw her in her bareness today,
a bareness I had never looked in.
It lay 'neath the surface,
her heart and her soul,
no matter the cover of skin.

And a great true awak'ning
came into my realm,
an awak'ning which burned in my mind,
    that this uncovered bareness
    permeated awareness
    of totally different kind.
I saw 'neath her skin
as I looked down within,
a sight I was late to behold,
    a sight bringing me to a reality
    which the years now allowed to unfold.

So I stared at her heart,
and I stared at her soul,
    and the wonderment wormed its way in,
and my feelings were swayed
by this wonder arrayed,
    and I vowed I would stay there within.

POETRY

Lift up your mind,
lift up your heart,
lift up your spirit,
yea, your viscera,
and place them all
into a steaming cauldron
of delicious word-soup—
poetry!

Let the verbiage be the broth,
the vegetables the adjectives,
the nouns the meat,
and the simmered whole
the final savory concoction,
the feat of art,
the music of the soul.

A MOTHER COOING TO HER CHILD

There are beauties rich and rare,
there is love beyond compare,
there are glorious views
in nature's many hues,
but none so sweet, so warm, so dear
as mother's loving voice so clear,
oh! Such a sound
so meek, so mild,
a mother
cooing
to her child.

DO/DON'T

A seeming quandary.
Do we do, or *don't* we do?

Damned if we do, and
damned if we don't?

When the two are sat
side by side in choice,
"do" always seems to win.
And why is that?
Habit could very well be a reason,
or even compulsion, force,
from an outside source,
but more commonly,
more importantly,
the "dos"
demand *desire.*

Let us here mention
the age-old adage:
"The road to hell is paved
with good intentions."
That old saw recognizes
the raw truth, which is,
to be perfectly blunt
and not so nice,
we will do as we *want,*
regardless of the outcome,
regardless of the price.

But don't get it wrong
about the "dos."

It is soooo much fun
to have it not *two* ways,
but *one.*

YESTERDAY, TODAY, AND TOMORROW

Today will be yesterday soon.
That's where all the todays go,
slipping into the past like zephyrs,
breezy encounters, furious flailings
at fleeting fancies,
guarded peeks at forbidden futures
which follow like night to new day
—tomorrow.

And so they come,
and so they go,
yesterday pushing today,
tomorrow urging today to end,
and send thrills, chills, or nils
through our waning time.

IMMERSED IN VERSE

Covered, as in a deep, deep pool, at bottom.
Immersed in verse, as inundated with the water of rhyme,
    leaving time and breath aside,
    only hiding deep,
    keeping rhythmic pulse alive.

Striving for the ultimate in self-expression,
    the pureness of poetry.

But who will reach so deep?
　　Who will plunge into creativity,
　　and fully immersed,
　　froth to the top
　　with a creation of art?

O powers that be,
　　please give to me
　　at least a glimpse
　　of such a treasured artistry.

A CHANGE TO BE

Life is change.
Change is life.
Change after change,
raining down our life-spout,
allowing us no out but to change,
to go with the tide, side to side,
front to back, threatening to crack
the very foundations upon which
our life has been built.

Now we cry,
"Is there no escape,
no refuge, no alleviation
from the constant progression,
regression, obsession
with never-ending change?"
Where to hide to no further abide it?
Cover up, and refuse to ride the tide
that wants to drag you, perhaps screaming,
perhaps dreaming, scheming,
from your complacent comfort
into change's discomfort?

Oh, now I have it!
Go with the ruthless waves of change;
submerge yourself into that
which is urging you on
to newness, to flights of fancy,
welcoming the chance to dance
to diff'rent drummer,
all the while a'passing winter's summer
into hopeful spring,
until the fall
determines all.

CHOICES AGAIN

They pass by regularly,
and always leave their mark,
so we would do well to
hearken to their call, and
exercise our will while
it's still willing to function.

Opt out.
Cry out.
Use your voice.
Make a choice.
Then, *live* with it!
Yes, *give* with it!
Never sorry.
Never worry.
Be *done* with it!

REALIZATION

And all of a sudden
in life it begins;
you forget all your sorrows,
forget all your sins,
and bask in the glories
that once passed you by,
the moon and the earth,
the sea and the sky,
the lovers you've loved,
the friends here and gone,
the daffodils, daisies,
the good times passed on,
and on the horizon
so wondrously clear,
the feeling of fateness—
your future is here!

ON THE OTHER SIDE OF THE MOON

Lovers spoon and croon on this side of the moon.
Space probes view the other side.
But where is the love there?

A song says, "Love is where you find it."
Is it to be found on the moon's other side?

On the near side is the man in the moon.
Is the woman on the other?
If so, how shall the twain meet for love?

The lovers lie above us in mystery.
But meet they where
in their vast separation's sea?

Perhaps the moon's center
provides the trysting place
for our potential lovers to enter
and occupy their mutual space.

And so our orb hovers day and night,
lighting both sides of our earth,
but keeping its dark secrets
at least temporarily at height
on the other side of the moon.

IF YOU WERE ME AND I WERE YOU

If you were me and I were you,
what in the world would then we do?

You'd hold yourself suspended where
no one could catch you by the hair
and pull you in to their caress
or mess up any tidiness
you had achieved through many a day
to cover all the other ways
you'd fallen short of aspiration,
and settled just for contemplation
of all the various things you'd do
if ever act should fall on you.

And there I'd be in my cocoon
a'singing up to shining moon,
forgetting all that's done below
by ev'ryone who finds it so
confusing that they sit and moon
and croon a tantalizing tune
that cuts through cloud to firmament
and hopes for something permanent

to hold so close at bosom's heat
that would allow my silent feet
to finally make a sudden stir,
while listening for the pleasant purr
that emanates between us two
if you were me and I were you.

And then, again, I say to you,
if you were me
and I were you,
we would be one,
instead of two.

CHOICE

The doctrine of "free will" absolves God of blame.
How could that same loving, merciful, just,
omnipotent, omniscient God allow the myriad
inequities, suffering, inhumanities
amidst and among his "creations,"
his "likenesses," his "same"?

The doctrine of free will explains it all.
We make the choices and inflict upon ourselves
all manner of ill.
Thus, it is *our* will that's involved,
not that of our beneficent Creator.

Now suddenly enters in fate, destiny.
And who determines our fate?
Who determines who it is
who waits at heaven's gate?

Move it up a little higher,
move it down a little lower,
let it be.
Choice after choice,
with no tiny voice to say
"*MY* will be done!"

So without God's will,
the question beckons still,
"What's over the *next* hill?"

EVERYTHING WILL WAIT

Yes, everything will wait.
Yes, even death and taxes
may be postponed.
But not fate.

Fate is written out for you.
Tempt it if you will,
ignore it if you will,
but it will have its way with you.

Fait accompli.
The fact is accomplished,
so resistance is useless.

So what to do about this insistence?
Nil, nichts, nada.

Live your life as it unfolds before you
and be thankful for its strife,
as well as for its surprises,
prizes, satisfactions.

Will it all wait?

All but fate.

IN A CHILD'S EYES

In a child's eyes all is wonder,
nothing there to put asunder,
all is new.
Grappling with the strangeness all about,
without doubt to stifle inquisition,
no position to defend,
all is newness without end.

Loving mother offers breast
when the angel needs its rest,
daddy picks up where the momma's leaving off,
tossing child up in air aloft,
child no fear that daddy's arms and hands not near.

Day by day our little one
greets the morning's rising sun,
drinking all the wonders in,
never having time to sin,
using minutes 'til the waning sun
has disappeared,
and child's
day's
done.

A CAROL OF THE WORD

Here's a carol of the word,
trying not to be absurd.

Rising from primordial slime,
just in time for Christmas.

All the masters, Bach and all,
answered their best instinct's call;
out from them came songs of love,
meant for those who watched above.

Noah's beasts could only hear
all the lays of yesteryear
falling on benumbed ear
from benimbled intellects
pouring out their sound effects.

Who would think those melodies,
rose engendered by the seas
on to land, and thence to skies,
that firmamental panorama
stretching out from out to gamma?

Now all those who fain would damn it
haven't run the great one's gamut.

GOING?

When I look around about me
and survey the people there,
I keep wond'ring, "What about me,
am I living here or there?"

Then I say right to myself,
"You seem here, and you seem there,"
all dependent on the moment,
all depending what I dare.

If I dare to seek the reaches
beck'ning me from far-off space,
then perhaps the destination
is the one that's called
"my place."

WHEN I BEGAN TO SEE THE LIGHT

Along about age forty, fifty, or so,
I began to see where all things ought to go;
that is, I started to be a "nature detective,"
beginning to put things in proper perspective.

At thirty, completely involved in my work,
most everything was cranial,
perceived as all "brainial."
It was all in my head,
in and out of my bed,
and I missed all the wonders
that passed by my eyes,
the glint of the moon,
the shapes of the skies.
And suddenly, feeling invaded my frame,
and from then on, my life was not ever the same.
In lieu of my mental meandering's amplification,
I now saw the beauties of nature's creation.

So now when I lie on my back in the pool,
I revel in feeling. No longer a fool,
I'm awash in the wonders invading my being,
and close to aghast at the new things I'm seeing;
my newfound mentality's fires of ignition,
a'lying there waiting for my recognition,
and oh, it's sooo great now to put things so right,
to sit back, relax, and at last see the light!

A PRICE TO PAY

Just as for every season
there is a reason,
for every happening,
occasion, experience,
there is a price to pay.

Whether willing or unwilling,
it will be paid!
And paid perhaps in agony,
longing, unfulfillment, incompleteness,
all the thwarted desires.

Oh how avoid this trial?
Deny denial.
Pay the price, whatever be,
and set the mind,
the spirit, the viscera,
free.

A SENSE WITHOUT A NAME

There is a sense, a feeling, an awareness,
not sensual, as are the five oft-listed,
not extrasensual, as is Extra Sensory Perception,
but yes, it *is* perceptive.
It perceives *beyond* the sensual, beyond the extrasensual,
into a magic land of awareness, so nebulous,
so other-worldly, so incapable of definition,
so "far out," so charming, enchanting,
so *different* as to escape all recognition,
except within the innermost recesses
of the enquiring psyche.
It transcends the mind;
it even rises above or beyond all *thinking,*
beyond all recollection.
So *sense it,* all ye, *sense it* and *live,*
live through the tempest of its permeation!

A DEARTH OF REGRET

Regret?
Why?
What's done is done,
and may be done again.
If I regret, I'm stupid.
So, stupidity.
Stupid before, on this earth,
stupid again, in my dearth.

"I did it again, and I'm glad"?
Perhaps I am.
Perhaps I'm sorry.
But if I'm sorry,
I regret.

Regretfulness makes no sense,
has no mirth.
The die is cast,
and at the last
it will be,
again,
on earth.

BEAUTY FROM ABOVE

God's beauty surrounds me,
it glows in the day,
it drives all my cares
and my sorrows away,
infuses my being,
appeals to my fire,
and plumbs up the depths
of my hidden desire.

Clustered clumps of autumnal color,
painted shades in varied hue,
nature's gift to me and you.

At evening the hues are as rich as before,
the trees' former fire has recessed into more
of subdued forms of richness pervading the scene,
and we thrill to the wonder of all we have seen.

BEYOND INFINITY

Everything that happens is preordained.
You don't believe it? Believe it!

When sparrow falls, it falls out of purpose.
And what is this "purpose"?
Ah, there's the rub!

Not a subhuman, but a superhuman ordained it.
And that "super" is beyond all thought,
beyond all recognition, cognition,
identification or fancy.
Superior to "super,"
ethereal past the ether,
mysterious beyond all mystery,
magicful beyond the magical,
infinite beyond the infinitesimal.

So we purport not to presume the purpose,
but sit back in our solitariness
and satisfied, glory in the knowledge
that we do not know.